Bettye's Blue Sea Chest

As told to Kenneth Knott

Elizabeth "Bettye" Adams Noyes

For information:

Kenneth Knott
Labiche Publications
6 School Street #15
Mystic, CT 06355
860-536-9615
knottk@aol.com
http://www.labichepublications.com

ISBN: 1539384144
ISBN 13: 9781539384144

Printed in the United States of America

Dedication

Dear Dad: Most of this book is about mother's side of the family. They seemed to be the writers. I haven't forgotten you. I am dedicating this book to you because you gave me the greatest gift anyone could give another person.

You gave me emotional support and encouragement, and you gave life meaning. Most importantly, you always believed in me. Thanks, Dad. Love, Bettye

Bettye and her Dad, Henry A. "Del" Adams, ca. 1940

This is the story of my nickname – *Bettye.*

In my first-grade class, there were two girls named *Elizabeth.* The teacher flipped a coin to see which student would be called *Elizabeth* and who would be called *Betty.*

From that day forward, I became *Betty* Adams. At High School, there was a beautiful blonde girl who spelled her name *Bettye.* I liked that spelling, it was unique.

After she graduated, I took that spelling of my name – *Bettye* (teenage charisma).

Contents

Part One – A Letter is Forever

In today's world there seems to be a general reluctance to using any correspondence that isn't instant. We have instant messaging, e-mail, texting, voicemail and video. The act of hand writing correspondence seems so outdated and slow, that we summarily discount it as outdated. Yet, without the written letters we are losing parts of our soul, the histories of families and stories that make us who we are today. I am one of the lucky ones whose family saved several generations of correspondence. Marcel Proust said the only true voyage of discovery is not to visit other lands, but "to possess other eyes, to behold the universe through the eyes of another." Here is my story:

Imagine sitting on an old wooden box, on a hot, humid August day, surrounded by personal effects of ancestors who lived some 200 years ago. The place was the "Smith Homestead" in Canterbury, Connecticut. I vividly remember the pungent smell of old wood, the spidery look of cobwebs laced in among the corners of the windows at each end of the attic; and the wasps as they hummed about overhead.

Dripping with perspiration running into my eyes, I was excited to discover what surprises awaited me. I sensed that I was about to unearth pirate gold. My dear Aunt Dorothy was with me, and generously gave me her time that hot summer, as we shared the spirit of discovery in that hot, stuffy attic. We were surrounded by many generations of furniture, dishes, bric-a-brac, old school books, teacher's notes, and family letters.

This saga was unfolding in the 1960s. One of the biggest surprises was a pen and ink sketch of the United States of America, dated 1820, and found under the eaves. The map was in perfect shape, except for a brown spot in the Atlantic Ocean where a mouse family left its signature.

When Uncle Henry E. Smith died, he left the Smith Homestead to me, with the wonderful contents, including the Blue Sea Chest.

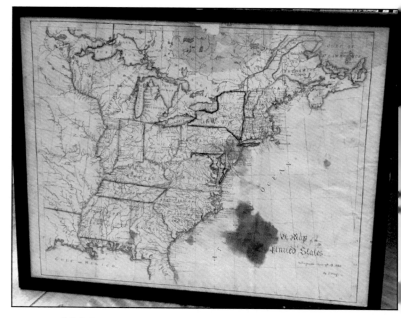

1820 map, drawn by hand by C. W. King

Uncle Henry with "Smokey," 1950s

Back in the stuffy attic along with the dust, humidity, and stale air, Aunt Dorothy and I began investigating the boxes, crates, and chests, stacked under the eaves like ghostly skeletons. Among them were 4-poster beds, spinning wheels, flax wheels, barrels, chairs and chests. Blowing off the top of the old chest I'd dubbed the Blue Sea Chest, I created a feathery cloud of dust. We were sneezing, coughing and laughing all at the same time, as we wiped grimy tears from our eyes. I slowly opened the lid, and initially discovered scruffy leather bound books, and well-worn family Bibles. As we gently lifted them out of the chest, we discovered stacks of letters tied with bits of string or blue ribbon.

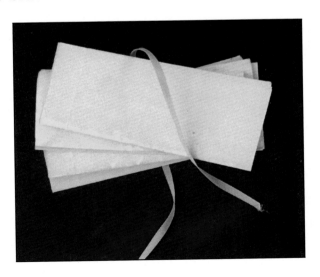

/e soon realized that these letters, dating from
ꜱ 1892, were written by my ancestors, the Smith and Lasell family members. As I scanned the letters, I read about the family's activities, some daughters moving west into New York State, the sons to Vermont, and of their hardships and tragedies.

Every day at noon, we took a break from exploring the attic and went to my mother's house for lunch about five miles away, in the village of Hanover. She always served us iced tea, delicious egg salad sandwiches, and cream cheese with olive sandwiches cut into perfect little triangles. (I can still taste them.) I was excited to tell my mother about the treasures we discovered, but she was not surprised to hear of them. She knew the Smith family _saved everything_.

The thought of those sandwiches began a replay of the memories in my head like a video. My past came alive again. Uncle Henry lived in the "Smith Homestead" until he came to live with my mother in 1945, after my father died. Uncle Henry and my mother kept the Smith Homestead as a family retreat and vacation place, fully furnished, with oil lamps, well spring water, and a big cast iron cook stove which burned wood or coal. Continuing the tradition, I frequently used the Homestead for Girl Scout overnight excursions and church youth retreats, until it was sold in the 1970s. The house was a magical place. I say "magical" because the sight of the old wash room, the water pump, and furniture and pictures were still in place as if a family had just left for the day. This atmosphere of the house began to reinforce the family bond created by the letters.

The Old Smith Homestead, 1960s

Then another memory popped into my head. I remember, as a teenager, riding my horse Spot up the dirt road to Aunt Nettie's house (my mother's older sister) near the Smith Homestead. It was a bright shiny spring day. I saddled Spot, who was white with black spots. Why else would he be called Spot? He was gentle and pranced along the road as if he were showing off. We took a circular route on dirt roads, which was about five miles away. Whenever I rode up to Aunt Nettie and Uncle Nelson James' little Colonial Cape style house, she would appear on the top steps, usually with a bag of cookies for my trip home.

Bettye on her horse Spot, mid 1930s

Aunt Nettie was a tiny woman with a sweet face, always smiling. Her hair was in a bun on the top of her head with wisps flying about her face. Inside the house a big black stove stood in a dark kitchen in front of a boarded-up fireplace. There was also a table and tin pans for washing dishes. Just outside the kitchen door was the well, with a bucket and rope wound on a wooden roller for drawing water. I remember letting the bucket down into the moss-lined well, and winding it back up full of water. The water was always cold and thirst-quenching.

In my teenaged heart, I sensed that Aunt Nettie lived a hard life – with a husband who was an "Old Woodsman" and "Old Raconteur" with spellbinding stories and experiences, but he was not very helpful with domestic chores. Most of the housework fell to Aunt Nettie, as it was considered "women's work." They had no electricity and washed their clothes in a wooden tub on the kitchen table. To help insulate the room, instead of wall paper they covered the walls with paper plates. Their three living sons were adults, and two had moved away. One son, Arthur, never married, and stayed home. How sad it seemed to me, that he lived such an isolated life with no horizons to explore. I vowed not to be caught up in such a way of living. However, their smiles and warm embrace emanated a sense of quiet contentment.

When Aunt Dorothy and I finished the sandwiches and iced tea, we returned to the attic in the Homestead. As we rummaged through the attic, I remember the stories Uncle Henry told us about the people who lived there. The "Horribles Parade" was a

July 4th family activity in the early 1900s, before my time.

The "Horribles Parade," ca. 1900

At holidays as I was growing up, such as Christmas, and the 4th of July, our extended family would gather at the Homestead. We had a big tent in the front yard with a table full of treats, like homemade clam chowder, and ears of corn dripping with butter.

We had watermelon, of course, for other summer fun. We ate through a whole rind of melon, pushing our faces through the circle and spitting out the seeds. Our chins were dripping with juice.

Bluff Point camping, watermelon fun, ca. 1924

Uncle Frank had an old Stanley Steamer at the Homestead, in the barn on blocks, and the wheels in the air. It didn't run, but we loved playing on it, sitting on the wheels. Suddenly, the video stopped running in my head, as I began to ponder what to do with all these letters.

It took me over 50 years, to sort all the letters chronologically and into family groups. I learned that my mother was a bit of a coquette, and loved to dance. She also loved homemaking.

I found an old album as I was sorting through my treasures, with photos of my parents from early days in their relationship, in the early 1900s.

Mother, Edith J. Smith (Adams)

Father, Henry A. "Del" Adams

My father was a chauffeur for the Ladensacks, a wealthy family in Boston who were involved with the S.S. Pierce & Co., a fine food company. He drove their Pierce Arrow to bring my mother home to Canterbury, before I was born.

My father driving the Pierce Arrow in the early 1900's. The family was proud of him.

My oldest daughter inherited the domestic skills of my mother, which unfortunately, skipped a generation – me.

One of my mother's favorites was a pie crust with a fern design. Priscilla creates the design using a regular dinner knife.

Fern design drawings and pie crust
made by my daughter, Priscilla

I saved the letters from my mother when I attended Wheaton College in Norton, Mass., from 1936-1940. I majored in English and a minor in art history. Someone recently asked why I saved the letters from my mother. My only answer was "It's in my genes." Almost all of the written correspondence I received at college was from my mother. My father once wrote asking if I had broken my left arm because I had not written home. (I am left-handed, so I think he was doing a bit of scolding.)

I discovered the "Smith Homestead" in Canterbury, CT, was the center of local industry during the 19th century. An early 1868 map of the town shows that it was called "Smith Mills" located on the fast flowing "Little River" at the junction of four roads. It was an ideal location with a busy water powered saw mill, a shingle and picker stick mill, a blacksmith shop, a woolen mill, and a carding mill. Here the Smith family prospered until the rapid advance of the Industrial Revolution. My Uncle Henry Smith wrote a poem published in 1958, in the Norwich newspaper, to commemorate the Smith Homestead, which read in part:

Memories of What Used to Be at The Old Homestead

As I sit on a bench that is on a
    bank quite high
And watch Little River go rushing
    by-
Memories surround me like a dream
And I think of things that now
    can't be seen.
The old woolen mill which is no
    more-
Where blacksmith shop stood whose
    anvil would ring
When folks around town horses
    drove in
Now stands a fir tree quite tall and
    bushes around – that's all.
The house on the hill where different ones lived
No longer is there, but instead a
    thicket of trees
    and bushes grow everywhere.
Doing for others has always prevailed
In this old home in the dale.
Money was made, but money was
    spent
To give to others more happiness.

As years go by and I am no more, may this spirit remain
for evermore.

The poem has several more stanzas; however, as I read it I realize that I could be writing the poem about the old homestead today. It expresses exactly how I feel about the homestead today, 59 years after it was written. It is like the ghost of "Christmas past," as it began to open my eyes to who I was, where I came from, and provided a thread with the stories and the letters, and MY life.

I carted this mother lode of letters, deeds, and estate papers with me, taking up space whenever I moved. My children were constantly rolling their eyes at this seemingly silliness of mine; yet they accepted my quirk with grace.

Unfortunately, I did not find an adventurous sea Captain's story, or unsung war heroes of the Revolutionary War, War of 1812, or the Civil War.

What I found were stories of families who lived ordinary lives with courage, determination against all obstacles whether separation by death, distance or the elements: love of family was their core value. One of my female ancestors, Desire Smith Lovett, told the story of how she and her husband George, ventured out from Connecticut to western New York State to homestead in 1838. The trip was by steamer from New London to New York City, and then on another steamer to Albany, NY. They wrote about being frightened by the burning cinders landing on the deck from the boilers as they steamed up the Hudson River, and their difficulty with the commercial banks in Albany for not accepting their paper money from Connecticut banks. After Albany, they continued their trip on the Erie Canal barge. They ended their journey in Palma Center, NY, near Lake Erie, PA. In her letter, Desire told a story about their fellow travelers, immigrants from Germany venturing to start a new life in America. These voyagers were an object of curiosity because they dressed differently, ate differently, and spoke differently than they did.

Mrs. Lovett wrote home to Ichabod Smith, her father, in Canterbury, CT, in 1838: "So, we looked at them - they (the immigrants) looked at us – we saw them cook, grind coffee, and boil rice. Cucumbers were cut up, and put in with potatoes and onions with milk. The mother and father would place these children on the deck and feed them from their dishes of coffee without milk, with the bread wet in it. They seemed to like their little babies – they would kiss their feet and would sit flat on the boat and knit."

Clearly, travel was not easy in those days, but they were not only determined, but succeeded despite monstrous obstacles.

we went out on the town path to see what discoveries were
to be made we were directed to a boate that contained
Germany people in number one hundred and ten and to
my surprise I bed them both and see them cook it was
the greatest sight that I ever beheld I could not understand
there language any more than I could the geese when feeding
there is never any thing make me more pityful than I did
to see human beings that was smart that I could not make
understand or word at any rate a little minister that travelled
all away from Albany went out with us he tried to
understand but we ... we looked at them they looke
cucumbers into ... cook grind coffe boile rice cut up
to make any ... sick to look at them with it was enough
mother would place there children before them on the
ground and fed them from the ... them on the
without milk with the bread wet in it tin dishes of coffe
no bonnets or shoes on set it did ... quick as where it new
clean thy deemed to like there little babes they would kiss
feet likewise there but they would sit flat on the boat
and knit I could ... any thing about the heathens before
Jeffrey would ... left at that place went to Jed Smith
they ... the boat sundry pedadish come with them
to meet part where ... the minister ... herd three sermons
starled at midnight ... tuesday at the Spencertown
I was tired a glad ... was about sick when we reached Parma
I have now recovered a ... much better live when we left
I do think that the climat agrees with me
we arived in safety nothing disturbed the whole journey
cost us but 10 dollars the freight three twentyfive the weather has
been extremely warm and dry we have not herd any rain for
nearly three weeks the dust is so fine it seems like ashes it flys
all over the fences city tres and grass looked so green that it looked
I gure to see people were cutting the third crops of grass when the
wheat comes in very light it is now two dollars per bushel potatoes
are very scary will hild are found with nothing in them apples
plenty likewise plums I eat more than a bushel my self a few
peaches I have been a visiting to day ... we have had some
grapes as big as a hazel nut or larg pees I cannot tell all ...

Mrs. Lovett's letter, Parma, September, 1838 – page 2

...to brother Jefferys yet I have been expecting since it was fairly new work to... they were going to hire & told them to hire me if any body for George had so many places in view that I thought best not to be in a hurry they think that he is married so they put him up to any price one place he has the refusal of they will determin this week and probaly move next week. George spend the Sabbath with us and visits us once a week besid which makes it honey moon with us yet as the old saying is however I have not seen him since Monday morning and think that he will be surprised when he comes to find that Mrs Arnold... Connecticut this week he was here I think he would... some of... you must excuse untill we get to keeping house he... we get settled I send you a news paper and date it for... takes the york... the same that... Wheeler takes so we have the... reading with us as with you the irish man said he was not thinking of that but far as he had come it was... here as in Ireland. as for as I have come I do realize that I am so far from home perhaps I may be home sick yet I have not had any symptoms. I wish brother Jason would take this bill and see if it pass there and if it will send a sorwich if convenient he come cut a peace of the paper the size of the bill out of a sheet or paper then do it up as a letter then it will be safe or it will risk it if you cannot pass it and loose it you need not send any money if it... good then send it in a letter. to direct you letter... to George and to Sienna corners Monroe county that is a little ways from... Jefferys... if I am... will know where I am perhaps I... will say by this time that I have writ enough... unless... more... write... and let me know the result and how you get along. so I will drawe to a close I hope you will not think much about me and worry about me when I am so cheerful. the Lord has prospered us thus for many many are we... commit ourselves to his care and trust in him that all may be for the best. I bid you all good by Give my love to all enquires.   Desire S. Lovett

it is so dry that two young men went a gunning and by shooting set a lot of brush and... on fire yesterday. I was reading in a paper that... two old women were haying and smoking until they were at work the... burnt in their hand... reading from the paper.

Mrs. Lovett's letter, Parma, September, 1838 – page 3

These letters introduced me to travels and tales I used later in role playing at Mystic Seaport as Mrs. Captain Caleb Reynolds, the wife of a clipper ship captain aboard the N. G. PALMER, living in the year 1876. Mrs. Reynolds used many of the stories contained in these letters, making the 19th century come alive for 20th century visitors.

Me as Mrs. Captain Caleb Reynolds, 1990s

I discovered that my mother and her older sister taught in the local schools, in the early 20th century. I found many of their lesson plans and teacher's notes, illustrating period essays, cursive writing exercises and conundrums, which I subsequently used at Mystic Seaport teaching about "Schools of Long Ago" (1876-1890). The Chest also contained many Bibles. The Bible that Mrs. Reynolds carried in her reticule belonged to Marcia Lasell, dated 1843. It gave the Captain's wife, Mrs. Reynolds, an air of authenticity, and a believable character when she could open the flyleaf and point to the date – 1843.

Being a curious sort myself, and inquisitive about the lives of people and how they lived, I looked forward to countless tales in the next group of letters. Transcribing these letters over the last 40 years, has been like eating potato chips, not stopping until they are all gone. Reading their own handwritten words about their lives was fascinating to me. Oh, those women writers! How I wished they had written more about their personal feelings and thoughts. As pragmatic New Englanders, they were primarily concerned with seemingly mundane topics, such as chores, sickness, neighbors' families, homesickness and death, with long eruditions of apology for not writing sooner. After all, this was their life.

Earlier, I mentioned an 1820 hand drawn pen and ink map retrieved from the homestead, of the United States of America and its territories, signed by C. W. King, who was married to Chloe Lasell. Mr. King was a professor at boarding schools in New York and Florida. He was also a Director of the Glen Haven Water Cure Facility, ca. 1866, a spa in Glen Haven, New York, a facility for the lingering or chronically ill. The treatment included introducing having healthy eating habits, sleeping with the windows open, and bathing in ice water. Lucy Lasell Smith wrote about the improvements in her health, and sense of rejuvenation she felt after being at the spa for several weeks.

In the attic, we also found an old atlas of Connecticut towns with the map of Canterbury, in 1868. It showed the location of the Smith Homestead at the intersection of crossroads at the bridge over Little River called "Smith's Mills." I had the map framed as a bit of family history.

The letters recalled many childhood memories for me, but one that stands out the most, is that of Uncle Henry's Hanover General Store and Post Office, in Hanover, where I grew up. I especially remember the pot-bellied stove, the mail boxes, and the ubiquitous homemade checkerboard on a small table.

The Old Hanover General Store-Uncle Henry with Minnie Lord Rose, store clerk and postmistress, and a small girl, beside the delivery truck, ca. 1920-1923

This was the "Old Hanover General Store," built sometime in the 19th century. I have memories from the age of 6-8 years old there. My friends and I would remove the cork lining from the bottle caps, place the now empty cap on the front of our sweater, and push the cork into place inside the sweater to hold the cap in place.

The New Hanover General Store, 1927

The "New Hanover General Store," was built in 1927. Uncle Henry was the owner of this store and the postmaster. He carried canned goods, cold cuts, cookies with pink marshmallow, coconut sprinkled on top, and of course, the tempting big glass case filled with penny candies in many little rectangular glass dishes. Inviting me were licorice, jelly beans, Milky Way bars, hard candy, lollipops and more. I can still smell the meat as he sliced the cold cuts. He would then tear off a piece of brown paper from the paper roller on the counter, to wrap the cold cuts. Then, from overhead, he pulled on a big ball of string, cutting off a piece to tie the package. I remember his pals were always hanging around the store. What fun it was to ride with Uncle Henry in his red pickup truck to deliver groceries to his customers. How important I felt, and it was exciting!

Another memory that came floating back to me was when we went clamming in 1934 or 1935, at Bluff Point, in Groton, CT, which faced Fisher's Island. I was working during the summers as a waitress in Westerly, but lived at our cottage at Bluff Point. I recall going down to the sand flats with my cousins as we looked for long neck clams. Armed with our buckets and shovels, eyes intent, looking for little pin pricks in the sand, and focused on the little hole to see if a little water spray might come up. If it did, we went down on our knees and dug with our hands and bingo. We would find a long neck clam, "oh and be careful, their shells are thin, and we don't want a cracked one." How yummy they tasted after steaming in the big kettle over the fire – on the shore – as we pulled them out of the shell, dipping them in sweet melted butter, popping them into our mouths. Yum!

Going quahogging was quite another adventure. Quahogs are hard shelled clams, that live off shore and are covered in mud. When I was a teenager, my mind was on boys, and I would not miss a chance to be with them. Margaret, my best friend, and I, agreed to go quahogging with our teenage heartthrobs of the moment, Donald and Russell. We used Donald's rowboat and once away from the shore, the four of us found a shallow area with a muddy bottom. We threw the anchor overboard and prepared to dive in after the clams. Following the boys, we went in the water which was about up to our waists. We had little buckets tied around our waist. And, we had to tread around in the mud and dig with our toes until we felt the hard shell of a quahog. Then we would dig it out with our toes or dive down to retrieve it. Bringing it to the surface didn't bother me, but horrible creatures might nibble at my toes down there such as a big blue shell crab or one might step on the spiky tail of a horseshoe crab. What courage and foolishness we could muster just for a couple of teen age boys. The clam chowder was worth it, though.

Bill Noyes helped me at Bluff Point, with my chore of bringing water jugs from the well. I will never forget he was 14, two years younger than I was, and the age difference then felt so big. Happily, things changed later.

As part of my research, I came across a quote from William Faulkner:

"The past is never dead, it's not even past."

As I look at the contents of the Blue Sea Chest, and my childhood memories, I understand what Faulkner meant. Although many of these letters and documents were over two hundred years old, composed by ancestors whom I never met or even heard their names, they are present in my everyday life.

One such "past which is not even the past" is the story of the fern on the apple pie. The memory of watching my mother draw a lovely fern leaf with a knife on the top crust of an apple pie survives today by my daughter, Priscilla, and my six-year-old great granddaughter, Maya. The memories we carry with us – especially when we have an "authentic" memoir, are to be passed on through generations. It surrounds us with feelings of connectedness and remembrance. Sometimes it is a fern leaf on an apple pie crust, a recipe, a wood carving, a painting, a sculpture, or a quilt. I was fascinated with reading – in their own words and handwriting – of how they were part of my heritage.

History provides remarkable insights into our lives, causing us to keep in perspective that people don't change that much. The experiences of our forefathers, the challenges they faced, even the trivial ones, provide us with insights for our modern dilemmas. Those early New Englanders realized that family and community tied them to one another, which built a support network when life's trials arose.

I hope my story helps demonstrate that love for and helping others is a deeply meaningful experience. Keeping that perspective helps us to curb our selfish thoughts, when we realize that extending hope and compassion is the most meaningful yet seemingly trivial response to life.

Is there someone in your life to whom you have been meaning to write, to tell a story, recall a family memory, share an experience, or tell them that they are loved? I do, and cannot catch up!

Part Two - "I Have Come That They May Have Life and That They May Have It More Abundantly" (John 10:10, *King James Version*)

This Bible verse was inscribed over the library portal when I was a student at Wheaton College in Norton, Massachusetts. (It is still there today.) Yes, I was impressionable when I first read it. I was only a freshman then, but it seemed to be speaking directly to me, Elizabeth Adams.

Why me? (Great question!) My classmates were drawn to write the great American novel, to be a teacher, a lawyer, or a scientist. In a sense I envied them, because their goals in helping mankind were clear, and the career path was clearly defined. My path was ill-defined with no clear focus or track, only a general sense of helping other people define their dreams and flourish with their strengths. I just wanted to learn about everything and experience college life.

This quote at the Library resonated with me, because my mother was kind, gentle, and warm. Her smile and graciousness welcomed all who came to her door.

Adams home, Hanover, CT, 1920s

My mother and father raised me to be thoughtful, hospitable, and to enjoy life. By being so generous, they brought a fullness to the lives of others and consequently to me, as well. My upbringing may be a clue as to why John 10:10 made such an impact on me.

Our family church, the Hanover Congregational Church, was a central part of life. I attended there as I was growing up, and later in adult years, with my family. I was christened as an infant, with water from the Jordan River, and at age 12, was given a Bible to have for my own. My father was a Deacon, and my grandparents attended regularly, too. I was active in youth group meetings, a good social time. We were all live wires, trying to get others to join us.

Hanover Congregational Church, 1920s

In my teens, I went to UConn, which was smaller back then, to a youth conference week with a number of speakers. I recall as clear as a bell, a candlelight service there, where we sang rousing hymns. We walked out of the Chapel holding our candles in the silent, quiet beauty of so many lighted candles moving in a heavenly line, in the dark night. On the walk back to my dormitory, I had a forever emotion that this would be my life.

My father ran his own business, Adams Motors Co. in Baltic, CT, and was interested in the social, community and political issues.

Adams Motor Co., Baltic, CT, 1917

In the middle of World War II, in 1942, my father and I were sitting on the rocky ledge in front of our cottage at Latimer Point, looking out on Fishers Island. I told my father how upset I was about all the violence and people dying in the war. He pointed to the stars in the sky and said that people are like the stars, everyone has a purpose, and none will be forgotten. What he was telling me was we are all unique, and we each have a purpose in life. Find your joy and you will shine as another star in the galaxy, and no one will be forgotten.

This inspired me to seize every waking moment, to meet new people, and explore new worlds. I believed life should be about joy, adventure, and fun, as it always was when my family got together. I clearly remember the story hour with Mrs. Stone, the minister's wife, who lived next door. She read us stories of missionaries helping others in foreign lands. I was in grade school when I made my career choice to be a missionary, primarily because I loved to travel and helping people was a nice idea.

When I attended High School, I had to ride the bus to and from home. I had many friends in High School and had an unending desire to reach out beyond my Lilliputian world, to discover more horizons of learning and social connections. Yet I was self-conscious, afraid to raise my hand in class, hoping the teacher would not call on me to answer a question. I had a burning desire to get over my shyness and be more self-assured. I never will forget Miss Talbot, a history teacher in high school, and her deck of cards. These were not ordinary playing cards. Each individual card had the name of a student. She would shuffle the cards and then select one to see who should be chosen to reply publicly to the class question. I would freeze up inside when the shuffling began. I thrived best on the casual interaction that comes from spontaneous meetings with others, not the formal give and take in a classroom.

After college, I went to the Hartford Seminary School of Religious Education, where I studied teaching skills and youth leadership. My father said that I would never earn a good living working in that field, and suggested I engage in social work instead. But I was more concerned with my newly found interests in working with children and young people. I received my Master's Degree in Education and quickly thereafter, received an assignment as Director of Religious Education at Wellesley Hills Congregational Church. A year later, I was offered a job as a teacher in a brand-new program, called Pioneer Valley Council of Weekday Religious Education, centered in Northampton, Mass. Classes were held in several little towns, up and down the Connecticut River. Students were released from school to go the nearest church for instructions.

No longer could I resist the persistent Bill Noyes, his wonderful disposition, and easygoing manner. He never gave up on me, after asking me to marry him since age 15. We were married in 1946, and my family grew with the birth of my three children. However, my creative imagination was always at work, leading me to many new adventures. Some of these were an extension of my childhood activities, such as organizing the Feather Club (getting entrance with a feather), the Pollyanna Club (for ages 10-14, with entrance for doing a good turn, such as helping carry wash for your mother). Later, as an adult, I established Camp Horizon, an outdoor camp for inter-racial campers, in 1973, and the Hanover Barn Art Center, in 1974-1979.

The brochure for the Art Center read in part: "... Explore the world of creative expression. The Hanover Barn Art School offers you a place to broaden your horizons through drawing, painting (and other art forms). The undiscovered capacities in every person's mind are well worth exploring, not only for personal fulfillment but to enrich the lives of all those around us." That mission pretty much summarized my life's ambition.

... the world of creative expression. The Hanover Barn Art School offers you a place to broaden your horizons through drawing, painting, sculpture, music; and it brings together the artists and craftsmen who can act as your guides in this adventure.

The undiscovered capacities in every person's mind are well worth exploring, not only for personal fulfillment but to enrich the lives of all those around us.

Elizabeth Adams Noyes

Elizabeth Adams Noyes
Director

HANOVER BARN
ART SCHOOL
248 Main Street   Hanover, Connecticut 06350

Class art set up and student painting

Discover a world...

My family and my mother's family, provided a nourishing ground preparing me for a life of helping others find happiness and enjoyment in life. Nevertheless, I was nagged by the question, "Why me?" Why this course for my life? Why did it feel so natural? It wasn't until I inherited my mother and uncle's Smith Homestead that I found a partial answer.

The first had to do with the Homestead itself. It was a 19th century farm house that had very little updating over the years. I could not part with the house, so I decided to use it as a retreat and church camp for youth groups. The goal was similar to that of the Art Barn, but also included developing and training future leaders while they learned about history, developing relationships, and of course, having fun.

My favorite memory of working with the Brownie Girl Scouts, was taking them on hikes looking for fairy houses. As we searched the woods, we talked about fairies we already knew like Tinker Bell. I would say "Keep eyes sharp for dead tree stumps with lots of holes, and soft green moss under a pine tree. Wouldn't moss be just fine for carpets? Little grasses standing up straight with 'fringy' tops could be shade trees." For furniture we found that acorn tops make sturdy chairs; a mushroom with a round top a great table; a walnut shell makes a cozy bed; and fallen oak leaves were useful for tents and canopies. The girls quickly caught the imaginary vision, and began hunting for or building fairy houses. My daughter, Priscilla, loves to create a "Story book" fairy house for Maya and Diego, her grandchildren.

Those who visited the Homestead loved living back in time. (Well, not all of them.) I enjoyed teaching the children about life in the 19th century and employing long lost survival skills, such as building a wood or coal fire in the iron stove, and learning how to carefully light an oil lamp. They seemed to relish this experience and at the same time, they learned more about themselves. Slowly, the letters became less about words and more about messages from my ancestors. I can almost hear the voices of Laura, Lucy, Ellen, Desire and Jerusha, when I read their letters. I truly believe when my father referred to the stars in the sky, that he also meant that they represented my ancestors, who had a message for me about what's important in life.

Dante Alighieri wrote in his treatise on language "that though men and women must communicate with words, angels can talk to one another in silence." We learn early on, that we communicate best when we have as little verbal clutter as possible. Eerily, I had communications in my lap from my relatives with no verbal clutter, as Dante called it.

Now, this is becoming a Twilight Zone story. Is Dante telling me, that angels are trying to communicate with me? He must be crazy if he thinks......; but why do I have all these letters? Just like a feather duster is not a feather duster to a child, but a migratory bird from some far off exotic land. So were these letters to me, an apparition from the past.

This was getting serious. I then re-read many of the letters out of curiosity, to see if Dante's theory was all a hoax. But this time I read them looking not at the words, but at the message they were trying to communicate to me.

The letters, mostly written by women, talked about the way people lived, places and culture. They talked about the tenacity of the human spirit, the challenges to provide a better life and to understand why we as humans do what we do. The letters talked constantly about looking after one another, and expressing interest in their welfare. I learned that human nature doesn't change that much. Rarely were commerce or financial matters mentioned in the letters, only individual activities and ailments. Many of the letters were written during the Civil War, yet the only mention of the war was of a nephew in the Union Army stationed in Nebraska as a deputy clerk, and a distant cousin with the Navy, and how they were getting along. The only mention of President Abraham Lincoln was one line which read: "I wonder about this man called Abraham Lincoln." That's it. Nothing about his assassination. No discussions about politics, only about the health and well-being of the relatives.

Times were very difficult in the 19th century, yet there was virtually no complaining. They wrote about how they got along, how they helped each other, and how they were grateful for little things.

The angels were speaking out loud now. I had several generations of ancestors telling me what was important in life. It was not how big your house was, or your social status. It wasn't about family members signing peace treaties, building skyscrapers, or being a captain of industry. Gary Saul Morson, a noted Russian author, once wrote that "The important events are not the great ones, but the infinitely numerous and apparently inconsequential ordinary ones which taken together are far more effective and significant." My families told me that in reaching out to others while working at everyday tasks, causes us to reach beyond our relationship capacities, and thus enrich everyone's lives.

I once wrote: "Know what you are good at, build on your special talents. Experience new adventures to expand learning and growing into the person you want to be. Keep your aspirations high and determination strong. When roadblocks to your dream career get in the way, be flexible. Never underestimate the network of friends and people resources. Remember that you are unique. There is a place for your God-given talents in this world."

Our lives are the cumulative effect of each minute, each lunch, each interaction, and each experience. We are shaped by these seemingly trite exchanges where we find opportunities to develop character and find joy in our lives. The events that have the most impact on us are the ones we realize at home with our family. The lessons we teach our children, and the things we learn from them. Every moment matters, and nothing is really predictable.

The best portion of a good man's life: "his little, nameless unremembered acts of kindness and love."

Helping others to have life abundantly, is what it is all about!

Special Thanks

Amazing – the way God sends people. Someone who gave inspiration when it was so needed, my writer and friend, Ken Knott.

I've had the letters for years and was not sure what to make of them. Ken encouraged me to tell a story about them, by finding the thread, and asking me what they meant to me.

Ken helped me re-discover my joy for life, as seen through the years.

Acknowledgments

I would like to thank the following people:

My daughters Priscilla Noyes Ginnetti, and Susan Noyes, for their support and encouragement, Priscilla for the fern pie drawing and pie images, and Susan for the painting of the Blue Sea Chest.

Ellie Coffey for her help in typing letter transcriptions.

Donna Good, for her help with my personal history.

Betsy Pittman, Archivist, at the University of Connecticut Library, where the Lasell and Smith family letters are preserved, and can be researched.

Sandra Rux, Archivist and Curator, who shared her expertise in saving precious old letters, and helped me with mine.

Louisa Alger Watrous, for her faith, enthusiasm, and help in giving birth to this book.

Illustrations

Fern pie drawings and pie photograph by Priscilla Noyes Ginnetti.

Lovett [Correspondence from Parma Centre, NY, 13:16] Smith Family Papers, Archives & Special Collections, UConn Library.

Other illustrations from the author's collection.

References

Bible verse from the King James Version in the public domain.

Quotes used are in the public domain.

About the Author

Elizabeth "Bettye" Adams Noyes, October, 2017

Bettye was born in 1918, in Baltic, CT, to Henry and Edith (Smith) Adams, and was an only child. She attended elementary school in Hanover, CT, and high school at Norwich Free Academy, in Norwich, CT. She married William ("Bill") Noyes Jr., in 1946. They had three children: Susan, Priscilla and William ("Bill") III. She currently lives in Noank, CT, and will celebrate her 100th birthday in 2018.